Original title:
Love in the Greenhouse

Copyright © 2025 Creative Arts Management OÜ
All rights reserved.

Author: Gideon Shaw
ISBN HARDBACK: 978-1-80581-901-1
ISBN PAPERBACK: 978-1-80581-428-3
ISBN EBOOK: 978-1-80581-901-1

Petals of Promise

In the garden where romance blooms,
Silly insects dance in little costumes.
A ladybug winks at a wayward bee,
While daisies giggle, oh so carefree.

Two worms tell tales of their secret meet,
Trading stories down beneath the heat.
They wriggle and squirm, making merry alone,
In a world where love's full-grown… in loam!

Between the Tendrils

Vines twist and twirl in a cheeky embrace,
Giving the daisies a run for some space.
Thorns roll their eyes at the sweet, soft peas,
While the sun gets jealous, wanting some cheese!

Frogs croak serenades in moonlit disguise,
As the roots snicker low, playing the wise.
Petunias gossip, petals puffed with glee,
Saying, "Look at that squash, what a sight to see!"

Embrace of the Foliage

Amongst leafy arms, a parrot squawks loud,
As the flowers sway, proudly, they're crowd.
A chameleon grins, changing hue with the laughs,
As butterflies trade their most colorful halves.

Each vine plays tag, with a curious twist,
While the cabbage rolls in, all green and missed.
The bees throw a party, buzzing up high,
While the carrots complain, "We can't reach the sky!"

Secrets of the Sunlit Oasis

In this sunny patch, secrets take flight,
Bumblebees buzz with well-guarded bite.
Cacti shrug off the rumors so bold,
As they poke fun at the roses in gold.

Mice wear tiny hats, ruling this plot,
Prancing around, happy with what they've got.
The sun pats the leaves, and they giggle away,
"Catch us if you can, it's a botanical ballet!"

Echoes of Green Silhouettes

In the corner, fern's a flirt,
Where petals play hide and seek,
The sun chatters with a smirk,
While vines giggle, oh so chic.

Cacti roll their eyes with glee,
They'll never understand the fuss,
While orchids whisper tenderly,
'We're too cool to ride the bus.'

Romance in the Shade

Two pots bump, a friendly dance,
That sweet basil gives a wink,
Tomato blushes, thinks it chance,
But parsley's there, with spicy stink.

The sunlight peeks through leafy arms,
Chuckles at the playful crew,
As daisies flaunt their charming charms,
'Kind of hard to stay blue.'

Against a Verdant Backdrop

The ivy stretches, reaching high,
Chasing sunlight, oh what a race,
While succulents just sit and sigh,
'Forever in this slow-paced place.'

Bumblebees buzz a tune so sweet,
Trying hard to steal a kiss,
But flowers keep changing their seat,
It's quite the greenhouse hit or miss.

The Dance of the Delicate

A posy twirls, it takes the lead,
While ferns sway with all their might,
A flower shimmies, sure indeed,
Turning this full plant ball bright.

The orchids laugh, throw petals wide,
As sunlight dips in the fray,
Competing, who will be the pride,
In this leafy cabaret?

Shadows and Petals

In the garden, shadows play,
Two hearts dance in their ballet.
A petal slips, what a scene,
As I trip on a bean!

His laugh blends with a bumblebee's buzz,
Mirth in the air, just because.
We twirl around the carrot tops,
Until the giggles, they never stop!

Growing Together

Our plants are wild, tangled, and free,
Like our hearts, as silly as can be.
With watering cans, we splash and fight,
A playful splash that feels just right!

He holds a sprout, I hold a weed,
In this chaos, we plant the seed.
We jest and tease, oh what a sight,
While squirrels dance under the moonlight!

The Serene Sanctuary

A haven bright with foliage grand,
We laugh amidst the sunflower stand.
In sun-kissed warmth, we plot and scheme,
As butterflies flutter, we steal the dream!

Prune the leaves, give a little tickle,
Our giggles blend like a sweet tickle.
In this serene, leafy retreat,
We trade our pots for a playful seat!

Kisses Among the Kales

In rows of greens, we sneak a kiss,
Amidst the turnips, pure bliss!
A lettuce leaf falls; we burst out loud,
Striking poses, feeling proud!

With every pinch of herbal glee,
We whip up love, just you and me.
In the kale's embrace, we play and sway,
Finding joy in the simplest way!

Eloquent Growth

In pots so round, they tango and twirl,
With petals bright, they frolic and whirl.
A vine proposes, oh what a scene,
Two leaves entwined, a leafy routine.

The daisies giggle, the daisies flirt,
They splash with sunshine, though covered in dirt.
A sunflower winks, with seeds all aglow,
As butterflies dance in a clumsy show.

Heartfelt Harvest

Tomatoes blush, ripe on the vine,
They whisper secrets, oh so divine.
Cucumbers chuckle, a ticklish spree,
While carrots peek shyly, just wait and see.

Herbs share gossip, scents swirl in the air,
With rosemary teasing, a fragrant affair.
Chives poke a joke, with their green little hats,
While basil just snorts and relaxes, how 'bout that?

Ties of the Green

In this jungle chaos, a bromeliad sighs,
Swaying to rhythms of sweet, silly cries.
A cactus lies back with its prickly charm,
Saying, 'Don't worry! I'm safe from harm.'

Orchids look prim, with their elegant pose,
But inside they giggle at their smell of old toes.
The ferns are a riot, spreading joy, oh so vast,
While ivy declares, 'My tangled side's a blast!'

Delight in the Dappled Light

Sunbeams filter, like a garden ball,
Where violets chatter and lilies enthrall.
A hummingbird zips, all tickles and glee,
While a lazy slug dreams of becoming a bee.

The wind whispers sweet, playful little tunes,
As dandelions dance, beneath laughing moons.
Flowers exchange notes with giggles so bright,
Creating a riot in the dappled light.

Connections Rooted in Soil

In the patch where daisies bloom,
I tripped on roots, went boom!
The carrots chuckled, roots all tangled,
While ladybugs around me jangled.

The sunbugs danced on leafy greens,
While I tried out my best routines.
With every stumble, a flower smiled,
And critters wheezed, 'That was wild!'

The Dance of Blossoms and Breezes

Petals twirled in the playful air,
While bees buzzed with style and flair.
I thought I'd join in the whimsical spree,
But tripped on a vine, oh dear, not me!

The daisies giggled, 'Keep up the beat!',
As I tangled my feet, what a treat!
In our dance of blunders, we seemed quite spry,
Even the weeds gave a cheerful sigh.

Skin against the Thorns

I hugged a bush, thought it was sweet,
But thorns disagreed, oh, what a feat!
The blooms all snickered, petals a-flutter,
While I danced away, yelling 'What a shudder!'

A rose mischief found me, can you believe?
As I wrestled with vines that clearly deceive.
'Next time, friend,' they said with chortles,
'Choose a softer hug, and not our portals!'

Garden of Yearning

In the rows where dreams take flight,
I spotted a gnome, what a sight!
He winked at me with a cheeky grin,
As weeds wrapped around my chubby chin!

With creatures giggling in the sun's embrace,
I pondered if this was my rightful place.
Surrounded by blooms that blushed and swayed,
I found joy buried in every braid.

The Language of Blossoms

In the garden where laughter grows,
Petunias whisper secrets, I suppose.
Tulips giggle in the gentle breeze,
While daisies jest, 'Do you want some peas?'

Roses blush as they overhear,
'He loves me not?' Oh dear, oh dear!
Sunflowers wink, with heads held high,
'Just wait for spring, we'll surely fly!'

Nurtured by Nature's Embrace

Cacti ponder life without a drink,
'What's a thorn if you can't even wink?'
Violets plot to steal the show,
While daisies cheer, 'We just grow and grow!'

Beehives buzz with a gossip spree,
'Did you hear about that flower tree?'
With petals dancing in cheeky glee,
They hum a tune, 'Come sip with me!'

In the Shade of Petal Dreams

The fern felt cool beneath the sun,
'Am I a plant, or just having fun?'
Marigolds paint the air with cheer,
'Let's grow some mischief while we're here!'

Lilies smooth their petals bright,
'With a wink and nod, we'll steal the night!'
In secret corners, they'll conspire,
To prank the sun with floral fire!

Ferns and Fond Memories

In the cozy nook where shadows play,
Ferns recall tales of yesterday.
'Remember when we all danced in rain?',
They laugh out loud, 'What joy and pain!'

With each petal drop, a memory stirs,
'Did you hear about that bee who purrs?'
In the laughter of blooms, the whole world glows,
As they share their tales in leafy prose.

Shadows of Fragrance

In the corner, a flower sneezes,
Pollen swirling with whimsical breezes.
A bee buzzes in, looking for fun,
Swapping sweet glances under the sun.

A sprout whispers tales to the vines,
Gossiping tales of blooming designs.
Petals all blush, acting all shy,
As butterflies laugh, ready to fly.

A root pulls a joke, causing a giggle,
While veggies dance and do a little wiggle.
Sunlight pops in with a playful glow,
Tickling the greens, making them grow.

In this lush realm, joy's on the menu,
Plants link arms, without a venue.
Under the arch of leaves, so spry,
The greenhouse hums a whimsical sigh.

Vibrant Bonds

Tomatoes blush with a juicy grin,
Cauliflower hands doing a spin.
Zucchini wrestles with an eggplant,
They laugh so hard, they start to chant.

A daffodil flirts with a tall sunflower,
Seeking sweet moments, hour by hour.
While radishes roll in a giggly row,
Squealing delight as they put on a show.

Herbs bring sass, like a quirky crew,
With minty winks and rosemary's bloom.
Chickens cluck softly, joining the rhyme,
In this wild patch of verdant prime.

Pumpkins tell stories from days gone by,
With laughter that stretches up to the sky.
In this garden, bonds flourish and twirl,
Dancing together in the earth's swirl.

Vines of Affection

Grapevines tangle in a fizzy embrace,
While radishes blush, keeping the pace.
Sunflowers nod to the giggles above,
Sharing secrets like old friends in love.

Cucumbers glisten in a playful twist,
Basking in sunshine, oh how they exist!
Lettuce prances, greens rustling loud,
While peas joke around, feeling quite proud.

A shy sprout whispers to its stout friend,
"Did you hear what the daisies just did?"
The roses chime in with a cheeky grin,
"Flower power's a riot where we all win!"

Vines climb higher, joining the cheer,
Bursts of laughter filling the air here.
In this jolly patch, chaos takes flight,
Making the day all sparkly and bright.

Rhythms of the Flora

In the garden's heart, a dance begins,
Petals shaking, joined by grins.
Wiggling all night, with roots of cheer,
Taking the stage beneath the moon's leer.

Daisies do the twist, so sprightly and bold,
Bouncing with joy, never feeling old.
Lively marigolds join in the spree,
Offering giggles, setting hearts free.

The herbs start to hum a catchy tune,
While gnarled trees sway to the evening's boon.
Chickens clap along with a flappy delight,
As garden denizens dance through the night.

With laughter like raindrops, they all unite,
In this haven where flowers take flight.
The rhythms of flora play wild and free,
Painting the night with a jubilant spree.

The Heart's Eden

In a place where vines entwine,
Plants have secrets, oh so fine.
With pots of joy, they dance and sway,
Whispering dreams in a leafy ballet.

Cactuses wear their spiky crown,
While roses frown, cannot break down.
A sunflower winks at the shy little bug,
And orchids giggle, feeling snug.

Lettuce laughs in shades of green,
As tomato plants strut, oh so keen.
In a pot, a snail takes a seat,
Sipping on dew, quite the treat.

Hiding gnomes chuckle with glee,
Watching the chaos, oh what a spree.
In this garden, antics never cease,
Nature's jesters spread joyful peace.

Ferns and Whispers

Ferns flutter wildly, whispering low,
While shy mushrooms pretend not to glow.
In the shadows, a critter prances,
Sipping the dew, it takes its chances.

Petunias sigh as the daisies tease,
Claiming they're the prettiest with ease.
Beneath a leaf, a ladybug pouts,
Wishing her polka dots came with shouts.

The basil snickers, full of zest,
While thyme air-guitars, feeling blessed.
All the herbs join in a merry jive,
Not one can resist, oh how they thrive!

Vines twist together in cheeky embrace,
Giggling at the butterflies' silly race.
In this secret world, joy knows no bounds,
As nature plays, in laughter, it resounds.

The Hidden Garden

In the hidden nooks where the wild grows strong,
Petals gossip all afternoon long.
Bees wear tuxedos, buzzing along,
While marigolds hum a cheerful song.

A garden gnome sips herbal tea,
Discussing the weather with a bumblebee.
Cabbages wobble, sharing a joke,
As peppers proclaim they're the hottest bloke!

A butterfly flirts with a brush of pink,
While parsley asks, "What do you think?"
Lilies giggle, swaying in time,
To the rhythm of verdant, charming rhyme.

Hiding behind pots, the ladybirds cheer,
"Stick together, let's spread good cheer!"
In this patch of mischief and glee,
Plants party hard, wild and free!

Flora's Embrace

In a twist of flowers, secrets reside,
Petals laughing, attempting to hide.
Chubby bumblebees play peek-a-boo,
While daisies swoon, feeling brand new.

Tulips chuckle in a rainbow line,
Saying to each other, "You look divine!"
Violets tease with a soft little nod,
While dandelions boast, "We're the real prod!"

An old watering can spills silly tales,
Of wandering plants with adventurous trails.
Pansies giggle, rolling in the breeze,
Planting joy as they aim to please.

As the sun dips low and shadows stretch,
The greenery whispers, no soul to sketch.
In this floral realm, laughter will bloom,
Filling the air with sweet, silly perfume.

Sprouting Hearts Under Glass

Two seedlings giggle in the sun,
A shy petal blushes—oh, what fun!
With watering cans filled to the brim,
They splash like children on a whim.

A quirky worm joins the jittery dance,
Twisting and turning, taking a chance.
The gardener's chuckle fills the air,
While two daisies plot to win the fair.

Cabbage gives sage advice with a grin,
Saying, "In this patch, it's a win-win!"
The tomato winks, ripe for a thrill,
Creating a scene that's hard to distill.

The sun sets low on this leafy space,
As two peas bicker in their tight embrace.
But beneath the glass, it's clear as day,
In this garden giggle, love finds a way.

Enchanted by Nature's Whispers

Beneath the leaves, where secrets bloom,
Ladybugs share a bit of gloom.
The sunflowers orchestrate a cheer,
While vines eavesdrop, lending an ear.

A wandering bee starts a silly race,
Buzzing around with a funny face.
"Can blossoms dance?" asked a playful fern,
While daffodils giggle, taking their turn.

The soil is rich with jokes untold,
As roots entwine, both young and old.
A caterpillar dons a tiny hat,
Swaying to whispers, just like that!

As evening falls, they share a laugh,
Counting the stars, their silent path.
In this world of green, the fun will grow,
Among tender shoots, a warm glow.

Vines of Shared Secrets

A vine whispers secrets to a shy sprout,
While comical snails play hide and shout.
"Let's hide from the rain, under this leaf!"
And giggles erupt, bursting in chief.

A dandelion shimmies in the breeze,
Jokes about clouds tease the leaves of trees.
"What would you say," to a leaf in a spin,
"About joining a race? Come, let's begin!"

Fresh petals blush as they share a glance,
Two crickets croon, instigating a dance.
The bamboo sways, making jest of the show,
While the garden watches, enraptured below.

As nighttime descends, the fun's not through,
With fireflies twinkling like laughter anew.
In this tangled riot, joy weaves a thread,
For every heart knows the tales that are said.

Cradled Among the Greens

Nestled closely, the seedlings conspire,
Exchanging whispers, igniting a fire.
A wiggly worm spins tales so absurd,
Chasing away clouds with each silly word.

The roses chuckle with sweet, pointed thorns,
While dancing gladiolus show off their horns.
"Come join our party!" invites a tall bloom,
As the mushrooms giggle, dispelling the gloom.

With sunshine spilling across every face,
Each leaf in motion finds its own pace.
The carrots dream of a comedic play,
Where each sprout shines in its own quirky way.

As night drapes the garden, laughter still flows,
From petals to roots, everyone knows.
In this cradle of green, joy's seeds are sown,
Where absurdity thrives—everyone's home.

The Caress of Sunlit Leaves

In a quirky patch of sun,
Plants whisper secrets of fun.
Cacti blush in the warm light,
While the daisies dance at night.

Lettuce giggles in a whirlwind,
Carrots wishing they could blend.
A tomato's crush on a pea,
It's an odd love recipe!

Sunflowers spinning, oh so tall,
Wonder if they'll ever fall.
Caressed by breezes, they sway,
Hoping to steal hearts away.

In this leafy world of cheer,
Every plant wishes to steer.
Bees buzz around with delight,
Join the fun under moonlight.

Entwined in Flora

Two vines tangled, quite a sight,
Prancing around in sheer delight.
A daisy pinching a sprout,
Whispering, 'Come, let's dance about!'

Petals flutter, oh what a tease,
Jack-in-the-Pulpit joins with ease.
Lily pads plotting schemes so sly,
To float away and touch the sky.

Butterflies having a wild ball,
As the drapes of ivy enthrall.
In each corner, laughter blooms,
Filling up the sunny rooms.

Nature's jesters in a play,
Making each moment a bouquet.
With every sprout, a cheeky grin,
In the garden, joy begins.

Where Fragrance Meets Devotion

In the air, scents twirl and laugh,
Rosemary winks on a grassy path.
Lavender wails, 'Pick me, pick me!'
While thyme just rolls, 'Oh, let me be!'

Chives are gossiping so loud,
Stirring drama in a crowd.
A mint leaf blushes, feeling bold,
With stories of fragrances untold.

Jasmine twirls, a fragrant tease,
Driving bees to squeeze with glee.
Just a whiff sets hearts on fire,
An aromatic, sweet desire.

As the evening scent unfolds,
Every flower watches and holds.
Blossoms join in fragrant fun,
In this game, they're all well-spun.

A Symphony of Green and Gold

A tangle of ferns composed in time,
Harmonizing breezes, oh so prime.
Banana peels slipping with flair,
While ivy's tango fills the air.

Basil leads in a sprightly jig,
Next to sage, doing a little gig.
Potatoes wink, hiding below,
In this garden show, there's a glow.

Peppers prance in vibrant hues,
Strutting their stuff with joyful views.
Onions shed tears of laughter bright,
In the dance of day and night.

Together they sway in a grand parade,
Nature's music, never to fade.
Dancing plants in a colorful fold,
A symphony of green and gold.

Embraced by Green Lights

Under the glare of fluorescents,
I dance with my ferns, quite decent.
With every twist, my heart takes flight,
Cacti cheer in the neon light.

Potting soil on my shoes for days,
Sipping coffee in plant-filled haze.
Succulents chuckle as they sway,
It's a daily botanical ballet.

My parlor palms gossip like teens,
Spying on me with leafy dreams.
They whisper secrets in a blend,
Of photosynthesis and pretend.

In this garden, humor blooms bright,
Sprouting giggles both day and night.
With nature's charm, I can't resist,
My plants and I— a silly twist.

In the Company of Flora

With daisies dressed in pink and blue,
I find myself lost in their view.
Pansies gossip, shaking their heads,
While I trample on daffodil beds!

Tomatoes blush when I come near,
Eggplant lobs jokes, loud and clear.
The herbs are all in on the joke,
Mint's breath is sharp; thyme just choked!

In this jungle of whimsical cheer,
I wear my gardening gloves, sincere.
But pruning shears have a wicked knack,
For snipping at laughter, not keeping track.

We dance beneath the sunflower eyes,
Swinging together with leafy sighs.
With dirt on my face, I twirl with glee,
It's a party of petals, just me and greenery!

A Love Like Ivy

Creeping vines wrap around my heart,
They tease with whispers— a leafy art.
I blush as they cling and pull me tight,
Each tendril's touch feels oh-so-right!

Budding blooms exchange little winks,
Plant pals giggle, "What do you think?"
As ivy climbs, I giggle back,
It's a jungle gym, not a heart attack!

My succulent date just gave a nod,
With prickly puns— oh, how they prod!
We're tangled in laughter, nature's jest,
Ivy's charm is simply the best.

In this riot of green, we become entwined,
Where humour and flora are perfectly lined.
With every bloom, our spirits ignite,
In this verdant world, it feels so right!

The Secret Life of Blossoms

Late at night, the petals convene,
Whispering stories, barely seen.
Daisies plot after dark, they scheme,
In the shadows, they share a dream.

Tulips trip with laughter and glee,
When the moon shines, it's their jamboree.
A daffodil tells a corny joke,
While the roses ruffle, almost choke!

Pollen parties are set to explode,
As bumblebees buzz on their decomposed road.
In this secret garden, under the stars,
Plants giggle and sway, no need for bars.

So here we dance, oh, how we play,
In the breeze, we chase worries away.
With a wink and a twist, life's blooms amaze,
The secret life's bright, in whimsical ways!

Blooming Affection

In corners of the tangled vines,
The laughter of the garden shines.
Petunias gossip, roses tease,
As bumblebees buzz with so much ease.

The sun tickles leaves, a playful jest,
While morning dew wears its sparkly vest.
Cucumbers dance in a leafy embrace,
Each sprout finds its rhythm, a silly chase.

Worms wiggle with glee underground,
While daisies sway to a joyful sound.
The veggies gossip, and the herbs chimed in,
In this patch of green, we all win.

With petals blushing in the sunshine's kiss,
Every sprout's joy is hard to miss.
In this wild garden, where fun takes hold,
Best friends grow here, stories unfold.

Nectar of the Soul

In the heart of the patch, where the bees buzz loud,
A swishing green carpet makes the flowers proud.
With butterflies flitting, all fancy and bright,
They flirt with the blooms, what a silly sight!

The tomatoes wear hats of leafy attire,
While peppers just dance, with wild desire.
Squashes and zucchinis share jokes by the hour,
Who knew veggies could have so much power?

Lettuce is laughing, its crunch full of glee,
The playful pumpkins whisper, "Oh, can't you see?"
In this patch of mischief where giggles abound,
Friendship grows stronger in the soil so sound.

Every fruit and leaf twirls with delight,
Filling the greenhouse with laughter at night.
Among the green friends in joyous ballet,
Is where the heart finds its quirky way.

Garden of Yearnings

In the corner where sunflowers stretch out wide,
The ridiculous rumors in petals collide.
They chat about bugs and the latest new trend,
In this wacky garden, all rules seem to bend.

Peas play poker in the soft, warm dirt,
While carrots debate who will wear the best shirt.
The cactus just smirks, with a prickly grin,
Watching the vegetables spin into a win.

Tomatoes compete for the brightest red hue,
While radishes blush, feeling shy in the dew.
Hyperactive clovers leap all around,
In this jolly garden, silliness abounds.

Amidst the sweet scents, oh how they bloom,
With laughter and fun, they fill every room.
In this whimsical space, joy takes its toll,
Welcome to the garden where hearts are whole.

Entwined in Flora

Within the tangle of green and glee,
The petals always giggle, quite carefree.
As hummingbirds joke, flaunting their flair,
The air's filled with chuckles, beyond compare.

The violets whisper secrets, oh so bold,
While ferns giggle softly as the stories unfold.
Sweet peas and beans, tangled in jest,
Welcome a rom-com for the plant-loving guest.

Radishes boast of their spicy cool flair,
While daisies plot pranks, without a care.
The willow tree sways, a laugh in the breeze,
In this garden of chaos, every heart sees.

Buds bloom with laughter each day anew,
Color the world with a vibrant hue.
In a patch of green where all bloom and play,
Life's fun is found in the quirkiest way.

Heartbeats in the Garden

In the garden, bees do dance,
They all have a style, with a flow and a prance.
Petunias gossip, tulips take a stand,
While daisies giggle, giving their hand.

Worms wear bowties, quite out of place,
While the sun's rays blush with a bright face.
Oh, the veggies chatter, sharing a jest,
With carrots competing for the best dressed!

Cucumbers chuckle at all of the fuss,
While spinach sings songs, we all ride the bus.
A butterfly winks, as sweet peas conspire,
In this vibrant mix, there's never a dire.

So here's to the laughter that blooms in the dirt,
Where the heartbeats thrive with a little flirt.
In this quirky estate, under sky's dome,
We find joy in the garden, our leafy home.

Embrace of the Ferns

In the shaded nook where the ferns hug tight,
A snail on a leaf plans a rave tonight.
Mosses wear party hats, sprucing it up,
While ladybugs sip juice from a tiny cup.

Squirrels bring chips, but forgot the dip,
While a wise old owl starts a gossip trip.
The mushrooms are dancing, a real toadstool ball,
With laughter that echoes and sprinkles through all.

A butterfly slips, gives a little twirl,
While the ants take bets on the next big whirl.
With ferns whispering secrets of old and new,
The whole green brigade knows just what to do!

So come join the fun in this leafy retreat,
Where giggles and green meet beneath the beat.
We'll sway with the breezes, dance in the ferns,
In this whimsical world, our spirit returns.

Growing Together Beneath Glass

In a house made of glass, things get a bit wild,
Cacti are sassy, a prickly child.
Tomatoes are blushing and feel quite grand,
While violets joke, 'We're the best in the land!'

With sunflowers pondering how high they can grow,
And peas in a pod giving truths that they know.
Watering cans giggle, splashing with flair,
While herbs in a chorus send out fragrant air.

But the basil's in trouble, a snail's on the prowl,
Yet the mint gives a wink, "I'll show you how!"
Together they flourish, with humor and glee,
In this glasshouse chaos, forever we'll be.

So let's raise a toast to the playful parade,
For the laughter we grow will never quite fade.
With every new sprout, we keep up the cheer,
In this hallowed glass place, with loved ones so dear.

Raindrops on Heartstrings

Raindrops tap-dance on the roof with a song,
While plants sway and whirl, singing right along.
A flower slips blush, 'It's just a little wet,'
Yet dances with joy and has no regret.

Bees wear tiny boots, splashing through puddles,
While frogs in a chorus hear their own cuddles.
When drizzles come drumming, the leaves clap their hands,
In this joyful orchestra, nature expands.

The peonies whisper, 'It's time for a rhyme!'
While clouds throw confetti, to keep up with time.
A raindrop winks softly, a playful tease,
As petals unite, in the rhythm and ease.

So let's roll with the drops, let our laughter bloom,
In this sprightly performance where giggles consume.
For when heartstrings are played with the rain as our guide,
We'll dance through the deluge, joyous and wide.

Glimpses of the Heart

In the corners where the ferns grow,
Whispers of fondness start to flow.
Petunias giggle, secrets shared,
Such odd matchmaking—who prepared?

The daisies dance, a sly little waltz,
While the orchids chuckle at our faults.
Sunlight spills, like clumsy hearts,
Wrapped in vines, the fun never departs.

A gnome almost kissed a shy pansy,
While butterflies laughed, feeling fancy.
Just like seedlings, the hopes they sprout,
With every misstep, they scream and shout.

Compost tales of romances wild,
Fertilized with dreams of a foolish child.
In this jungle of fervent delight,
Love blooms quirky, from day to night.

Moonlight Among the Blossoms

Under the glow of a quirky moon,
Cacti sway to a silly tune.
With petals prancing in the night,
Who knew flora could be so polite?

The tomatoes tease, in shades of red,
Blushing bright, they turn their head.
Laughter erupts from the blooming beans,
Making mischief in leafy greens.

At midnight, the tulips share a jest,
While the clovers take a nightly rest.
Dandelions whisper, secrets and dreams,
Sprinkled with giggles, bursting at the seams.

A moonbeam winks at a shy lilac,
Promises made, no hint of a black.
In the shadows, the fun takes part,
Nature plays tricks on the timid heart.

Untamed Sentiments

In the garden of chaos, hearts collide,
Where blossoms bicker with a twist of pride.
A sunflower mocks their floppy hats,
While the haughty roses roll out their mats.

Petals argue, who smells the best,
The daisies giggle, claiming the jest.
With butterflies buzzing, they spin and twirl,
In this zany world, love begins to whirl.

An errant breeze serves mischief, too,
As the lilies laugh, causing quite the stew.
Roots intertwine, in a tangled spree,
Every moment a giggle, wild and free.

Bulbs shoot up with quirky charm,
In this wrangled garden, hearts stay warm.
Nature's folly, with smiles so bright,
Creating a ruckus, day and night.

The Bower of Bliss

In a hidden nook where laughter grows,
Weed and flower chat, in rhythmic prose.
The violets snicker, it's quite absurd,
As petals gossip, oh what a word!

Beneath the trellis, a frog sings flat,
While dandelions joke about the chat.
With ladybugs roaming fancy-free,
Happiness sprouts from each tiny spree.

Jasmine winks at the rising dew,
Hearts flutter in colors bold and true.
Each stem's a tale, a jester's claim,
In this bower, joy is the name of the game.

Even the soil chuckles in delight,
As buds burst forth, an entertaining sight.
Amidst the greenery, fun takes root,
Here in the bower, bliss wears a boot.

Garden of Hearts

In a patch of dirt, I sow my dreams,
Tomatoes blush while the radish screams.
Two peas in a pod, they giggle and sway,
As sunflowers turn to watch the play.

The carrots dance with the leafy greens,
A patchwork quilt of vegetable scenes.
Radicals on roots, they have a ball,
Throwing their greens up in the fall.

The herbs chat gossip in a leafy hush,
While the pepper plants blush and crush.
With pots of laughter, they'll celebrate,
As onions snicker, it's never too late!

In this plot of joy, we plant our quests,
With veggie valentine hearts in their vests.
Let's grow a world where giggles ignite,
In this garden where everything feels right!

Whispers of the Wild

In the thicket where wild things prance,
Bumblebees twirl in a pollen dance.
Naughty nettles tease and poke,
While daisies giggle behind their cloak.

The breezes carry a zany song,
As critters frolic; they all belong.
A squirrel teams up with a bashful snail,
Together they spin a snappy tale!

Mushrooms wear hats, so stylish and tall,
They throw a party, inviting us all.
With every flutter, there's joy to unfold,
In whispers of wild, new stories are told!

With laughter blooming in the softest glade,
The sun shines brighter, no need to fade.
Nature's jesters, in a whimsical spree,
In this wild wonder, come laugh with me!

Bubbles of Floral Bliss

In a garden where blossoms burst with glee,
Petals shimmer, like bubbles in the sea.
Daffodils dance while the tulips tease,
With giggles and wiggles, they aim to please!

Floral frolics, what a sight to see,
Lavender laughing like it's meant to be.
Marigolds flit from spot to spot,
In this whimsical world, they're never caught!

Roses exchange jokes, petals all a-quiver,
While bees buzz in, making us deliver.
Hydrangeas nod to the rhythm of cheer,
In bubbles of bliss, there's nothing to fear!

As moonlight kisses the blooms so bright,
They waltz in the shadows, spreading delight.
In such a place where colors all mix,
The garden of giggles is a floral fix!

The Kiss of Dew

Morning light sprinkles a glistening dew,
A kiss from the dawn, fresh and new.
Ladybugs laugh as they slide and race,
In this magical world, they find their place!

The ferns whisper secrets, gentle and sweet,
While spiders spin webs that can't be beat.
With every droplet, they giggle and glow,
In the warmth of the sun, what a lovely show!

Petunias prance in their colorful attire,
And in every nook, there's something to inspire.
With a flutter and twist, they give their best,
In the morning's caress, life feels blessed!

As the dew slowly fades, the laughter remains,
In a garden of joy, where happiness reigns.
With every new dawn, let's lift up our cheer,
For a world full of wonders awaits us here!

The Language of Blossoms

In the garden, whispers bloom,
Petals giggle with perfume.
Roses blush at secret texts,
Tulips tease with playful contexts.

Bees are busy with their buzz,
Pollinating all the fuzz.
Sunflowers wink with golden cheer,
Nature's matchmakers appear.

Daisies dance in bunny hop,
While violets plot a flower shop.
Ivy's ivy league of vines,
Conspire with the pines for signs.

Every sprout a joke to tell,
In this verdant, leafy dell.
Laughter grows amid the blooms,
Nature's humor always looms.

Scented Confessions

Underneath the leafy shade,
Petals spill the truths they made.
A daisy's heart is quite a flirt,
While roses wear their thorns like shirts.

Lily pads share tales of old,
Whispering secrets, bold yet cold.
Orchids boast of their grand style,
Pansies giggle all the while.

In the breeze, the scents collide,
Each aroma takes a ride.
Jasmine tells of midnight calls,
While wildflowers throw garden brawls.

Garden gnomes with grinning grins,
Lurk around to catch the sins.
Every bud embarks on quests,
With funny tales that life suggests.

A Symphony in Bloom

In the garden, music swells,
Petals strum with fragrant jells.
A trumpet vine begins to sing,
While the lilacs gently swing.

Tulips tango, tango twice,
Pansies play the cards of dice.
Daffodils beat on their drums,
Insects join in with their hums.

The roses samba through the heat,
Sunflowers tap their happy feet.
Every stalk in rhythm sways,
Playing tunes in sunny rays.

The wind strums along the line,
This merry band, divine design.
Nature's laughter fills the room,
A symphony of joy in bloom.

Tender Roots

Underground where secrets hide,
Roots entwine and twist with pride.
Whispers dance beneath the ground,
Silly stories swirl around.

Worms are comedians in the dirt,
Tickling toes of plants with hurt.
Every sprout is in on the joke,
Sharing giggles 'til they choke.

Sinkers laugh, while twisters spin,
Creating chaos with a grin.
What grows above is just a ruse,
Down below, they're all amused.

Beneath the soil, they laugh and tease,
Finding joy in gentle breeze.
Tender roots with hearts so wide,
In the shadows, fun won't hide.

Whirlwind of Green

In a pot, a basil sings,
While the mint does silly swings,
The tomatoes plot their pranks,
Spreading joy in leafy ranks.

Cucumbers whisper jokes so sly,
Green peas giggle, oh my, oh my!
With each sprout, a chuckle bursts,
Nature's humor, truly firsts.

An ivy vine wears a funny hat,
While a rogue radish aims for that,
Lettuce winks with leafy grace,
As garden gags take root in place.

And as kale does a jig or two,
The sunflowers join with a whoop, woohoo!
In this patch, the fun won't fade,
In nature's jest, we're all remade.

Under the Canopy of Emotion

Under leaves, a squirrel's cheer,
Whispering tales that we all hear,
The ferns dance to a silly beat,
As butterflies flit on light feet.

A cactus grins in sunny glee,
While others joke, 'Hey! Look at me!'
The daisies blush; oh, what a sight,
As they twirl in a pure delight.

Bumblebees buzzing with sweet roars,
On nectar spills, they share their scores,
Jokes about flowers, oh, so witty,
In this garden, nothing's gritty.

Each leaf holds laughter, bursting bright,
In the shade where giggles ignite,
Nature's jesters in full bloom,
Creating fun while chasing gloom.

Shadows in the Aroma

In the corner, herb pots plot,
Chasing shadows, they frolic a lot,
Thyme is tickled, sage just sighs,
While cilantro dreams of tasty pies.

Noses twitch at the fragrant game,
Lilies and onions both stake claim,
Garlic with a grin, quite the tease,
Playing tricks on the gentle breeze.

Basil's flirting with the chives,
Counting all their kitchen lives,
Underneath the busy sun,
Their aromatic antics are pure fun.

In sweet scents, the laughter swells,
From garden echoes, the tale tells,
With each sniff, a giggle grows,
In the air, it happily flows.

Love Letters to the Earth

A dandelion writes a note,
In the wind, it starts to float,
Dear Earth, your soil's just divine,
I'll spread my seeds across the line.

The carrots giggle in their beds,
Writing rhymes in leafy threads,
O, how we adore your sun,
In this dirt, we all have fun.

Bees send greetings, buzzing loud,
Dancing 'round, so sprightly proud,
Tulips blush as cards are penned,
Stirring joy that knows no end.

The earth replies with a warm embrace,
In each sprout, a smiling face,
A potpourri of humor dear,
In the garden, all is clear.

Love's Tapestry of Growth

In a jungle of plants, we frolic and tease,
You're the sunflower, I'm the bees.
Trying to play hide and seek in the vines,
But you trip on the roots—oh, those silly times!

With pots full of laughter, we dance and we prance,
While watering love with a goofy romance.
Our blooms are a riot, in pots bright and round,
Who knew all this joy could be found from the ground?

The ferns whisper secrets, the leaves giggle too,
As we argue 'bout pruning—could I keep a shoe?
The tomatoes roll laughter, the peppers throw shade,
In this garden of joy, we've got it made!

And when we get tangled, oh what a sight,
With you by my side, everything feels right.
Planting our quirks in this vibrant decor,
In our patch of the world, there's always room for more!

Heartfelt Petals Unfurled

We've cultivated moments that tickle the soul,
Like growing a salad that's out of control.
You pull the wrong weeds, thinking they're gold,
And I can't stop laughing, this must be retold!

A rose with a twist, a daisy that sings,
You're the joker in bloom, oh the joy that it brings!
With mint leaves a-swaying, we dance in delight,
Each petal's a giggle, our future looks bright!

The watering can splashes, a drench on your nose,
As cucumbers chuckle, and the thyme just knows.
Your smirk's contagious; the basil's impressed,
In this quirky patch, we're forever blessed!

So let's tangle our roots in this fun little space,
Where weeds can't outgrow us, not even a trace.
With petals in chaos, together we'll thrive,
In this garden we share, oh, we're so alive!

In the Secret Garden of Us

Under the arch where the wildflowers bloom,
You tease the tulips while I shout out zoom!
In this secret patch where the butterflies play,
We giggle and tumble, such a wild ballet.

The carrots are hiding, the radishes peek,
I try to be quiet, but laugh like a freak.
Your garden hat's tilted, a sight to behold,
You're more charming than any pot made of gold!

With daisies for laughter and sunflowers bright,
You dance like a bee, and it feels so right.
Petunias are gossiping under the sun,
Oh, the joy of this patch, we've already won!

So let's plant our dreams, let's harvest the fun,
With each twist and turn, two hearts beat as one.
In the secret of us, where the wild things are,
We'll bloom a laughter that's never too far!

Shadows of Affection Play

In a patch of green where giggles unfold,
You tickle the daisies while the sun turns to gold.
As shadows stretch long, we dance on the grass,
The butterflies blush as our moments come to pass.

You hold a sweet sprout like a precious gem,
"Watch out!" I cry, "Better hide from the phlegm!"
The pollen is thick, and the humor is grand,
In this wacky garden, we've got quite the hand!

Through petals of pink, our laughter cascades,
With every small mishap, a memory's made.
Our friendship's a jungle, in bloom and in jest,
Each joke is a seed, and together we're blessed.

So let's frolic in sunshine, ignore the weeds' sighs,
With shadows of joy cast beneath sunny skies.
In this amusing patch, with a twinkle and sway,
We'll nourish our smiles and let our hearts play!

Rhapsody in the Rain

Droplets dance on the roof,
Little plants wearing hats,
With raindrops as their cue,
They sing to the cheeky cats.

Basil flirts with a sprout,
Tomato blushes with glee,
A lettuce shimmies about,
As it spins in jubilee.

Cucumbers whisper soft tunes,
While parsley laughs away,
The marigold hums to moons,
All in the wet ballet.

In puddles, worms twist and groove,
Earthworms wear shiny shoes,
The garden is in the mood,
For silly rain-dancing blues.

Sentiments in the Soil

Underneath the ground, they bicker,
Beans claim their turbo speed,
Beets say, 'We're here to flicker!'
With radishes planting a seed.

Compost speaks in hushed tones,
'This carrot's got some flair!'
While onions share their groans,
Saying 'We just make folks stare!'

With roots entangled in fun,
Together they pull and twist,
In their earthy, secret run,
A garden party they can't resist.

Laughter bubbles in the dark,
As earthworms wiggle and roll,
Each sprout gives a cheeky spark,
With nature's giggly soul.

Tapestry of Leaves

Leaves are dressed in bright hues,
A quilt of whirls and sways,
Ferns in a flirty muse,
Sway to the breeze's phrases.

Sunflowers stand tall and proud,
Spinning tales of the sun,
While daisies giggle out loud,
At squirrels that dance for fun.

Vines compete in a grassy race,
Trailing up the fence and wall,
In this leafy, lively place,
Everyone wants to sprawl.

The air filled with chuckles free,
As petals tickle the breeze,
While whispers among the trees,
Create a symphony of glee.

The Gentle Writings of Nature

Nature pens a silly tale,
With twigs and dainty leaves,
Pansies giggle without fail,
As the wind weaves through the eaves.

Mushrooms sport sassy hats,
Each one a quirky design,
Rabbits dance with their spats,
In this garden so divine.

Butterflies flutter and dash,
Writing poems in the air,
With colors that make you flash,
Like a breeze without a care.

Every flower's got a wink,
A secret code to be shared,
In this blooming, bright link,
All the critters have declared.

www.ingramcontent.com/pod-product-compliance
Lightning Source LLC
Chambersburg PA
CBHW070333120526
44590CB00017B/2868